PIANO ACCOMPANIMENT

MW00667281

BROADWAY FAVORITES

Solos and String Orchestra Arrangements
Correlated with Essential Elements String Method

Arranged by
LLOYD CONLEY

Welcome to Essential Elements Broadway Favorites! There are two versions of each selection in this versatile book. The SOLO version appears in the beginning of each student book. The STRING ORCHESTRA arrangements of each song follows. The supplemental CD recording or string orchestra PIANO PART may be used as an accompaniment for solo performance. The recording may also be used as a teaching aid in string orchestra rehearsals. The optional PERCUSSION book may be used with the FULL STRING ORCHESTRA arrangements. Create endless programming possibilities with the accompaniment backgrounds and any combination of instruments!

Piano Accompaniment Page	*Title*	*Correlated with Essential Elements*
2	Edelweiss	Book 1, page 34
4	Beauty And The Beast	Book 1, page 42
6	Circle Of Life	Book 1, page 42
8	I Dreamed A Dream	Book 2, page 30
11	The Phantom Of The Opera	Book 2, page 30
14	Sun And Moon	Book 2, page 30
16	Cabaret	Book 2, page 43
18	Get Me To The Church On Time	Book 2, page 43
20	Go Go Go Joseph	Book 2, page 43
23	Memory	Book 2, page 43
25	Seventy Six Trombones	Book 2, page 43

ISBN 978-0-634-01857-2

HAL•LEONARD®
CORPORATION
7777 W. BLUEMOUND RD. P.O. BOX 13819 MILWAUKEE, WI 53213

00868044

From THE SOUND OF MUSIC

EDELWEISS

PIANO

Lyrics by OSCAR HAMMERSTEIN II
Music by RICHARD RODGERS
Arranged by LLOYD CONLEY

37
53
61
69
opt.

From Walt Disney's BEAUTY AND THE BEAST: THE BROADWAY MUSICAL

BEAUTY AND THE BEAST

PIANO

Lyrics by HOWARD ASHMAN
Music by ALAN MENKEN
Arranged by LLOYD CONLEY

21
29
35
rit. opt.

Disney Presents THE LION KING: THE BROADWAY MUSICAL

CIRCLE OF LIFE

PIANO

Music by ELTON JOHN
Lyrics by TIM RICE
Arranged by LLOYD CONLEY

29
37
p
rit. opt.

From LES MISERABLES

I DREAMED A DREAM

PIANO

Music by CLAUDE-MICHEL SCHONBERG
Lyrics by HERBERT KRETZMER
Original Text by ALAIN BOUBLIL and JEAN-MARC NATEL
Arranged by LLOYD CONLEY

00868044

20
30
f
mp
mf
39
f

47
mp
mp
rit.

From THE PHANTOM OF THE OPERA

THE PHANTOM OF THE OPERA

PIANO

Music by ANDREW LLOYD WEBBER
Lyrics by CHARLES HART
Additional Lyrics by RICHARD STILGOE and MIKE BATT
Arranged by LLOYD CONLEY

00868044

f
dim.
mf
35
f
43
mf

f
51
mp
f

From MISS SAIGON

SUN AND MOON

PIANO

Music by CLAUDE-MICHEL SCHONBERG
Lyrics by RICHARD MALTBY JR. and ALAIN BOUBLIL
Adapted from original French Lyrics by ALAIN BOUBLIL
Arranged by LLOYD CONLEY

30
p
cresc.
41
f
mf
mp
rit.

From the Musical CABARET

CABARET

PIANO

Words by FRED EBB
Music by JOHN KANDER
Arranged by LLOYD CONLEY

mf
35
Slower
rit. e cresc.
43
Tempo I
cresc.
51
f

From MY FAIR LADY

GET ME TO THE CHURCH ON TIME

PIANO

Words by ALAN JAY LERNER
Music by FREDERICK LOEWE
Arranged by LLOYD CONLEY

27
35
mf
43
51
f

From JOSEPH AND THE AMAZING TECHNICOLOR DREAMCOAT

GO GO GO JOSEPH

PIANO

Music by ANDREW LLOYD WEBBER
Lyrics by TIM RICE
Arranged by LLOYD CONLEY

29
f
37
mf

46
53
mp
cresc.
f

From CATS

MEMORY

PIANO

Music by ANDREW LLOYD WEBBER
Text by TREVOR NUNN after T.S. ELIOT
Arranged by LLOYD CONLEY

00868044

31
2
2
39
f
47
mf
2
2
55
f
mf
mp
opt.

From Meredith Willson's THE MUSIC MAN

SEVENTY SIX TROMBONES

PIANO

By MEREDITH WILLSON
Arranged by LLOYD CONLEY

mp
31
39
mf
1.
mp
2.

f
53
mf
61
f